FINDING DINOSAURS
DIPLODOCUS

by Rebecca E. Hirsch

FOCUS READERS

WWW.FOCUSREADERS.COM

Copyright © 2018 by Focus Readers, Lake Elmo, MN 55042. All rights reserved. No part of this book may be reproduced or utilized in any form or by any means without written permission from the publisher.

Focus Readers is distributed by North Star Editions:
sales@northstareditions.com | 888-417-0195

Produced for Focus Readers by Red Line Editorial.

Content Consultant: Dr. David B. Weishampel, Professor Emeritus, Center for Functional Anatomy and Evolution, Johns Hopkins University School of Medicine

Photographs ©: Herschel Hoffmeyer/Shutterstock Images, cover, 1; alredosaz/Shutterstock Images, 4–5; Classic Image/Alamy, 6; Bains News Service/George Grantham Bain Collection/Library of Congress, 8; I Wei Huang/Shutterstock Images, 10–11; Piotr Wawrzyniuk/Shutterstock Images, 12; Matthew Martyniuk CC4.0, 14; Francois Gohier/Science Source, 17, 25; Elenarts/iStockphoto, 18–19; Wendy White/Alamy, 20; Corey Ford/iStockphoto, 23; Deposit Photos/Glow Images, 26–27; milehightraveler/iStockphoto, 29

ISBN
978-1-63517-503-5 (hardcover)
978-1-63517-575-2 (paperback)
978-1-63517-719-0 (ebook pdf)
978-1-63517-647-6 (hosted ebook)

Library of Congress Control Number: 2017948062

Printed in the United States of America
Mankato, MN
November, 2017

ABOUT THE AUTHOR
Rebecca E. Hirsch is a PhD-trained scientist and the award-winning author of dozens of books about science for children. She lives in Pennsylvania with her family and assorted pets.

TABLE OF CONTENTS

CHAPTER 1
Colossal Fossils 5

CHAPTER 2
Long-Necked Giants 11

CHAPTER 3
Studying Sauropods 19

DIGGING DEEPER
The Morrison Formation 24

CHAPTER 4
A Mysterious End 27

Focus on Diplodocus • 30
Glossary • 31
To Learn More • 32
Index • 32

CHAPTER 1

COLOSSAL FOSSILS

In the fall of 1898, wealthy businessman Andrew Carnegie opened his newspaper. He saw the headline "Most Colossal Animal Ever on Earth Just Found Out West!" The story told about an amazing discovery in Wyoming. It included a cartoon of a dinosaur peering into the tenth-floor window of a skyscraper.

A Diplodocus skeleton was displayed at the Natural History Museum in London, England.

Henry Fairfield Osborn discovered this Diplodocus leg in 1898.

Carnegie decided he wanted that dinosaur for his new museum in Pittsburgh, Pennsylvania.

The gigantic dinosaur was named Diplodocus. It was one of the largest dinosaurs ever found. Diplodocus had actually been discovered 21 years earlier. Benjamin Mudge and Samuel Wendell Williston found bones from a hind leg and a tail in Colorado in 1877. In the two decades that followed, more Diplodocus bones were discovered. But no one had found an intact skeleton.

After Carnegie read the newspaper story, he contacted William Holland. Holland was the Carnegie Museum's director. Carnegie told Holland he wanted a Diplodocus. Holland assembled a team of top fossil hunters. He sent them to Wyoming, where the latest Diplodocus had been discovered.

This skeleton was part of a display in Paris, France.

When the team arrived, they learned that only part of a leg had been found. So they began searching for more remains. On July 4, 1899, they discovered a huge bone from a dinosaur's foot. As they dug, they found more and more bones. A separate expedition in the spring uncovered another partial skeleton.

The bones were shipped by train to Pittsburgh. There they were reassembled into one dinosaur and put on display. Carnegie was delighted with the dinosaur. He paid to have plaster casts made. He gave the casts to several museums in Europe, North America, and South America. Diplodocus became famous around the world.

NAMING DIPLODOCUS

Paleontologist Othniel Charles Marsh coined the name Diplodocus. The name means "double beam." It refers to T-shaped bones on the underside of this dinosaur's tail. These bones helped support the tail. The first species of Diplodocus discovered was *Diplodocus longus*. Carnegie's dinosaur was a different species. It was named *Diplodocus carnegii* in honor of him.

CHAPTER 2

LONG-NECKED GIANTS

Diplodocus was one of the longest animals that ever roamed the earth. Some of these dinosaurs were 90 feet (27 m) long. Most of this length came from the dinosaur's neck and tail. Its neck was made up of at least 15 **vertebrae**. Together, they made the dinosaur's neck longer than a pickup truck.

Diplodocus weighed between 10 and 20 tons (9 and 18 metric tons).

11

This model of a Diplodocus shows just how long its tail could be.

A long tail helped balance the weight of the neck. The tail could be the length of a school bus. It had approximately 80 vertebrae. At the end, the tail tapered to a thin tip.

Scientists used computer models to study how the tail moved. Based on these models, they believe Diplodocus could whip its tail. This movement made a loud crack. Scientists are not certain how Diplodocus would have used this sound. Males may have used it to attract females. Or it could have been a warning to other dinosaurs.

A SPINY TAIL

Fossilized impressions of Diplodocus skin were found in 1992. They showed that Diplodocus had small spines along its tail. The spines may have run from the back of the dinosaur's head to the tip of its tail. They were probably made of **keratin**.

Diplodocus walked on four sturdy limbs. Some early paleontologists thought Diplodocus walked with its legs splayed out, much like the way a crocodile walks. But there was a problem with this idea. In this posture, the giant dinosaur

DIPLODOCUS FEATURES

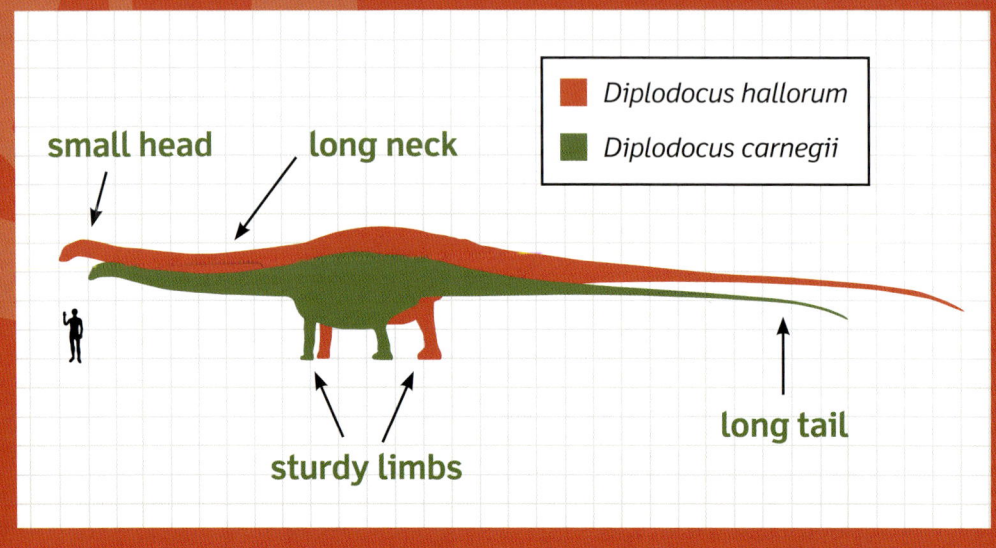

would have needed to stand over a large ditch to make room for its ribcage. Fossils of Diplodocus footprints were found in the 1930s. They showed that the dinosaur walked with its legs straight down, similar to an elephant.

For an animal with such a huge body, Diplodocus had a strangely small head. Its eyes were on the sides of its head. This helped it watch for predators. Scientists used to think its nostrils were high up on its forehead. They later discovered that the nostrils were down on its snout.

Diplodocus had small, peg-shaped teeth. As these thin teeth wore out, new teeth grew in to replace them.

Scientists believe Diplodocus could grow a new tooth approximately every 35 days. That is faster than other similar dinosaurs. Because its teeth grew at such a fast rate, scientists think Diplodocus probably ate **abrasive** food, such as plants with dirt on their leaves. This food would have worn the dinosaur's teeth down quickly.

Scratches on a dinosaur's teeth can also give scientists clues about its diet. As an animal eats, food and dirt leave marks on its teeth. Based on these marks, scientists think Diplodocus used its teeth to tear leaves off branches. It probably clamped its jaws on a leafy

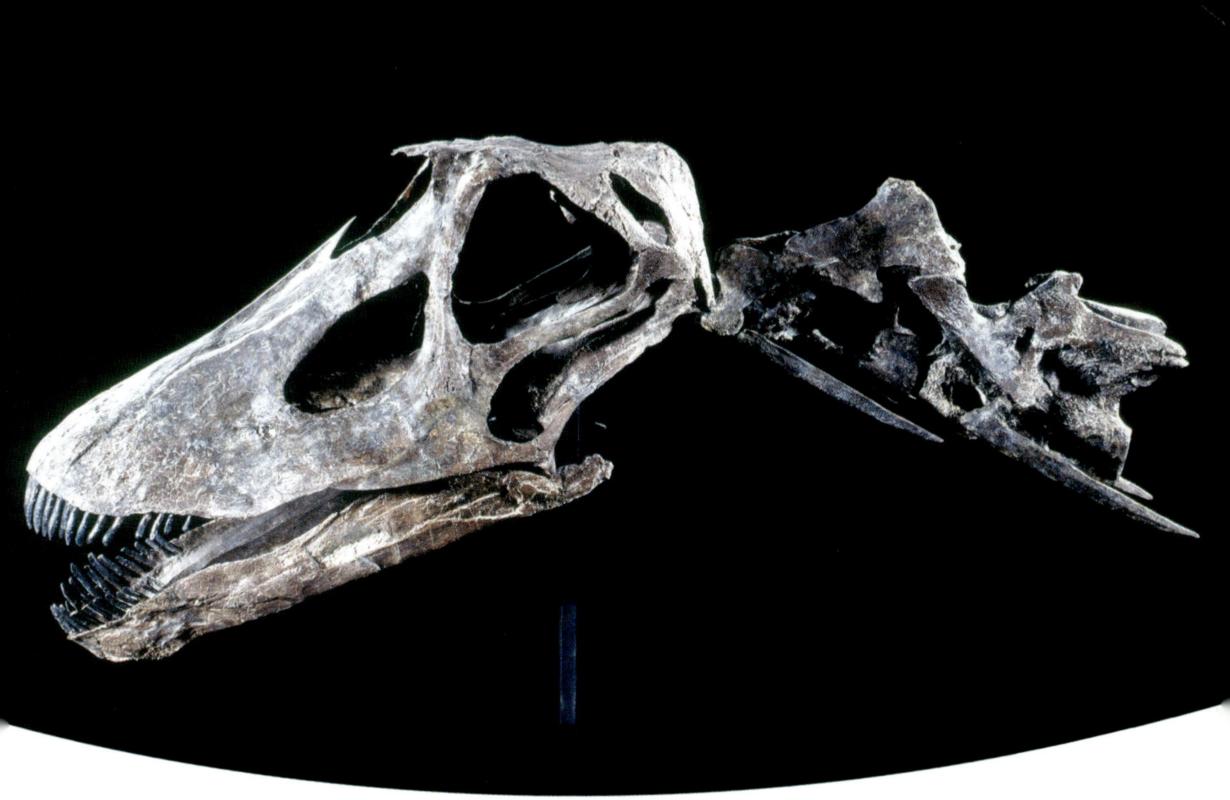

Diplodocus's blunt teeth had spaces in between them, similar to the spines of a rake.

branch and pulled its head backward. Diplodocus might have stood on all fours and raised its neck to eat from trees. Or, it could have reared up on its back legs and balanced on its tail. This would have allowed the dinosaur to reach leaves on high branches.

CHAPTER 3

STUDYING SAUROPODS

Diplodocus lived 155 to 150 million years ago, during the Late Jurassic period. The world was warmer at that time than it is now. The land looked different, too. The **supercontinent** Pangaea was breaking up into smaller continents. New oceans were filling the widening gaps between the land.

Dinosaurs such as Diplodocus were the dominant land animals during the Late Jurassic period.

This Diplodocus femur bone can be viewed at Dinosaur National Park in Colorado.

At this time, dinosaurs of all sizes were the dominant animals on land. Diplodocus roamed what is now western North America. Its remains have been found in Colorado, Utah, and Wyoming.

Diplodocus belonged to a group of plant-eating dinosaurs called sauropods.

SAUROPODS

All sauropods had long necks and tails. They also had small heads and sturdy limbs like the legs of an elephant. Despite its length, Diplodocus was not the heaviest sauropod. Its close relative was much thicker and heavier. An Apatosaurus that was the same length as a Diplodocus would have weighed twice as much.

Several other sauropods lived at the same time and place as Diplodocus. They include Apatosaurus, Brachiosaurus, and Camarasaurus.

These huge **herbivores** would have needed a lot of food. If they competed for the same food, some sauropod species would probably have gone **extinct**. Instead, scientists think sauropods ate different kinds of plants. This allowed several species to live together in one area and not run out of food.

Scientists are not sure exactly what Diplodocus ate. It might have eaten low-growing plants, such as shrubs and ferns. It could have eaten plants covered

Diplodocus probably swallowed its food by the mouthful.

by water along the banks of rivers or lakes. Or, Diplodocus might have eaten from **conifers**.

DIGGING DEEPER

THE MORRISON FORMATION

Diplodocus fossils come from a group of rock layers known as the Morrison Formation. The Morrison Formation reaches from New Mexico in the south to Canada in the north. It is made up of **sedimentary** rocks. These rocks formed between 148 million and 155 million years ago. They were laid down by ancient rivers and streams.

The Morrison Formation contains many fossils from the Jurassic period. The fossils give scientists a rich picture of what life in western North America was like during that time. The dominant trees were conifers. Plant-eating dinosaurs included several species of sauropods, as well as the armored Stegosaurus. Meat-eating dinosaurs included Allosaurus and Ceratosaurus. Smaller animals also lived in this region. They

Several Diplodocus vertebrae were found at Sheep Creek, Wyoming, which is part of the Morrison Formation.

included crocodiles, turtles, salamanders, frogs, and lizards.

CHAPTER 4

A MYSTERIOUS END

The Jurassic period was the peak for sauropods such as Diplodocus. By the beginning of the Cretaceous period, they became much less common. Then they disappeared from the fossil record in North America. Scientists do not know why this happened. One possible reason is that the environment changed.

Brachiosaurus (back) and Diplodocus (front) both lived during the Jurassic period.

If an animal cannot adapt to a changing environment, it will go extinct. By the beginning of the Cretaceous period, some types of conifer trees were disappearing. Flowering plants began to replace them. If Diplodocus depended on these trees for food, it could have died out, too.

Or, there might be a gap in the fossil record. The remains of most animals never become fossils. It is possible that Diplodocus was still alive after the early Cretaceous but very few of the animals became fossils. This would make the fossils very hard to find. Scientists have not yet found Diplodocus fossils from later periods. But a new discovery could

This Diplodocus skeleton was found in western Colorado.

change their ideas about when it went extinct.

There is still a lot that scientists do not know about Diplodocus. They do not know what color it was or if it made noises. They are not sure if it made nests. And they do not know the dinosaur lived in large groups. A new find may reveal more about these long-necked giants.

FOCUS ON DIPLODOCUS

Write your answers on a separate piece of paper.

1. Write a paragraph describing what Diplodocus looked like.

2. Would you rather dig for fossils or use a computer model to study dinosaurs? Why?

3. Where did Diplodocus live?
    - **A.** North America
    - **B.** South America
    - **C.** Africa

4. What might cause scientists to change their theory about when Diplodocus went extinct?
    - **A.** finding a Diplodocus fossil from the Late Jurassic period
    - **B.** finding a Diplodocus fossil from the Early Cretaceous period
    - **C.** finding a Diplodocus fossil from the Late Cretaceous period

Answer key on page 32.

GLOSSARY

abrasive
Causing wear or damage by rubbing or grinding.

conifers
Trees that have needle-shaped leaves and produce cones.

extinct
No longer living on Earth.

herbivores
Animals that eat only plants.

keratin
A type of hard protein that horns and fingernails are made from.

paleontologist
A scientist who studies the ancient past and the fossil remains of ancient living things.

sedimentary
Rocks that are formed when particles settle to the bottom of a lake or river, build up in layers, and turn to stone.

supercontinent
A large continent that existed in the distant past and split apart to produce the present continents.

vertebrae
The small bones that link together to form the backbone.

TO LEARN MORE

BOOKS

Alonso, Juan Carlos, and Gregory S. Paul. *The Late Jurassic: Notes, Drawings, and Observations from Prehistory.* Lake Forest, CA: Walter Foster Jr., 2016.

Knight, Sheryn. *Meet Diplodocus.* New York: Cavendish Square Publishing, 2015.

Woodward, John. *Dinosaur!: Dinosaurs and Other Amazing Prehistoric Creatures as You've Never Seen Them Before.* New York: DK Publishing, 2014.

NOTE TO EDUCATORS

Visit **www.focusreaders.com** to find lesson plans, activities, links, and other resources related to this title.

INDEX

Carnegie, Andrew, 5–7, 9
casts, 9
Cretaceous period, 27–28

extinct, 21, 28–29

fossils, 15, 24, 27–28

herbivores, 21
Holland, William, 7

Jurassic period, 24, 27

Late Jurassic, 19
legs, 14–15, 17, 21

Marsh, Othniel Charles, 9
Morrison Formation, 24–25
Mudge, Benjamin, 7

North America, 20, 24, 27

sauropods, 20–22, 24
skeleton, 7–8
species, 9
spines, 13

tail, 12–13
teeth, 15–16, 22–23

Williston, Samuel Wendell, 7
Wyoming, 5, 7, 20

Answer Key: 1. Answers will vary; 2. Answers will vary; 3. A; 4. C